I Want to Be a TRICERATOPS!

by Thomas Kingsley Troupe

illustrated by Jomike Tejido

PICTURE WINDOW BOOKS
a capstone imprint

I practiced my kickflips on the sidewalk as my little sister, Sarah, played with her toy dinosaurs.

"Raaar," Sarah growled, making her dinosaurs fight.

Then our older brother Jeremy and his friend Ben walked over. They kicked her toys down. "Now they're extinct!" Jeremy shouted. Ben laughed.

2

They made me so mad. "I want to be a Triceratops," I whispered, heading toward Sarah. "Then no one would mess with us!"

3

Believe it or not . . . I changed! I became Tracy the Triceratops! Horns grew out of my head. My mouth stretched and my skull felt like it weighed hundreds of pounds. I grew a tail and became heavier and stronger than ever!

And the best part? Sarah became a Triceratops too!

"Where are we, Tracy?" Sarah asked.

"The past, I guess," I said.

The world around us looked totally different. Trees and bushes I'd never seen before were everywhere. Small lizards ran past us.

Another Triceratops peeked out from some bushes.

"Hey," he said. "I've never seen you two before. I'm Trey."

A LOOOONG TIME AGO . . . Triceratops lived during the end of the Cretaceous Period. This period lasted from 145 to 66 million years ago. Other animals that lived at that time included Gallimimus, Ankylosaurus, and Tyrannosaurus rex.

5

We told Trey our names and followed him through the woods. I couldn't get used to how heavy my head felt. It was like carrying an armored tank on my neck! Having a stubby tail felt strange too. I could move it around. It brushed against trees and bushes.

The horn above my nose was hard to get used to as well. Anywhere I looked, I saw it!

"I need to get back to my family," Trey said. "They're in danger."

"Why?" I asked. "What's happening?"

The ground below my stubby feet trembled. Was it an earthquake? I stopped and Sarah looked scared.

"One by one, we're disappearing," Trey said. He hung his horned head in sadness.

The ground shook again. In the distance, I heard a loud, angry roar.

"We're being attacked," Trey said. "There's a hungry Tyrannosaurus rex on the loose. If we stick together, we've got a better chance of surviving."

I looked at Sarah's long, sharp horns. I couldn't imagine a big mouth like a T. rex wanting to eat us.

"Can we help?" I asked.

Trey led us toward the edge of the woods, then stopped us. "Don't move," he whispered.

We stopped in time to see a gigantic Tyrannosaurus rex attack. It snapped at a Triceratops with its awful teeth!

Sarah moved closer to me. "I don't want to get eaten," she whispered.

IT'S GREEK TO ME! The name Triceratops comes from three Greek words tri (three), keras (horn), and ops (face). Together they mean: "three-horned face."

"Let's go deeper into the woods," Trey said. "We should eat to keep up our strength."

I was a little hungry, but I didn't want to eat another dinosaur. Sarah and I watched as Trey bit into a big, thorny bush on the ground.

"Eat up," he said, with branches and leaves hanging out of his mouth.

TEETH TO SPARE! A Triceratops could have as many as 800 teeth in its mouth. Any time a tooth fell out, another would rise up to take its place. Imagine flossing all of those teeth!

I tasted some leaves from a smaller plant nearby.
They didn't taste too bad, but they were kind of chewy.

"Want the good stuff?" Trey asked. "Watch this."

Using the horns on his head, he pushed against a
tree until it fell over.

"The leaves on top taste best," he said. As Trey and
Sarah ate, I kept my head up. I kept watching for that
nasty big mouth, T. rex.

After eating and sneaking through the woods, we found Trey's family.

"What's that stink?" I asked, as Sarah and one of Trey's little brothers wandered off to play.

"Mom can't sit on her eggs to warm them up. She'd crush them!" Trey said. "Rotting plants help keep the eggs warm."

I saw half-buried eggs in the ground. The smelly, rotting plants formed a ring around them.

LEAVE MY BABIES ALONE! Many scientists think that Triceratops used its sharp horns to defend its young.

Suddenly, I heard a small voice call from the distance. "Tracy!"
I looked around, but couldn't find Sarah. Then I heard a roar.
I knew she was in trouble. I peeked through some thick bushes.
A T. rex stood roaring down into a deep gulch. Sarah and
Trey's brother were on a small ledge just below the edge of the
cliff. There was nowhere for the little ones to escape!

Since I couldn't run fast, I snuck up behind the T. rex. It made so much noise it couldn't hear me. When I was close enough, I rammed my horned head into its leg.

The T. rex roared in pain. I gave it a second nudge with my head. It tipped over and fell into the deep gulch. I heard it roar all the way down.

"That was close," Sarah cried.

"You see?" Trey said. "It's safer if we stick together."

"Yeah," I said. "We can put up a good fight until they get those big ol' teeth on us. Then it's game over."

We rejoined Trey's family. On our way back, we saw an older Triceratops eating some plants. His horns were worn and battered.

"Wow, you look like an old guy," Sarah said.

"Sarah!" I said. "What a rude thing to say." I was so embarrassed!

"She's right," the elder Triceratops said. "I've seen more sun falls in my life than I can remember."

As the old-timer lumbered into the forest, I thought about my neighborhood. Did Triceratops roam near my home millions of years ago? I wondered if there were old bones or fossils deep below the ground.

NO BONES ABOUT IT! Scientists have found Triceratops bones in Montana, South Dakota, Colorado, and Wyoming in the United States. Fossils have also been found in Saskatchewan and Alberta, Canada.

As we wandered through the woods, the area around us began to change. The dinosaurs faded away. Trees disappeared and our apartment building was back. Before Sarah and I knew it, we were ourselves again.

Her toy dinosaurs were scattered around the front steps. I helped her gather them back up.

As we played with her Triceratops, Jeremy and his friend came back again.

"Everyone knows the T. rex was the best dinosaur," Jeremy shouted.

"They had big mouths," I shouted back. Then Sarah and I charged toward them. "But they didn't stand a chance against a charging Triceratops."

As the boys ran off, Sarah and I smiled. Sometimes it felt good to stand up to the big guys!

19

MORE ABOUT TRICERATOPS

Triceratops is from the Ceratopsid family of dinosaurs. They are dinosaurs with horns on their heads, parrot-like beaks, and neck frills. Other Ceratopsids include: Achelousaurus, Protoceratops, Centrosaurus and Styracosaurus.

Some scientists think a two horned dinosaur named Nedoceratops was another species of Triceratops.

The largest Triceratops skull ever found was about 8.2 feet (2.5 meters) long. It was one of the largest known skulls among land animals at the time it was found.

Some scientists think that Triceratops may have had feathers all over its body. Little bumps on Triceratops' body might have been places where feathers or quills were once attached. An early relative to Triceratops, called Psittacosaurus, had a row of plumes running down the top of its tail.

Triceratops' head was so heavy the dinosaur most likely couldn't stand up on its hind legs. As a result, Triceratops was limited to eating low-growing bushes and plants.

Triceratops were among the last dinosaurs to exist before all dinosaurs (other than birds) became extinct at the end of the Cretaceous Period, 65 million years ago.

GLOSSARY

beak—the hard front part of the mouth of birds and some dinosaurs; also called a bill

extinct—no longer living; an extinct animal is one that has died out, with no more of its kind

frill—a bony collar that fans out around an animal's neck

fossil—the remains or traces of an animal or a plant, preserved as rock

gulch—a deep valley that fills with water when it rains

herd—a large group of animals that lives or moves together

life span—the number of years a certain kind of plant or animal usually lives

quill—the long, hollow central part of a bird's feather

species—a group of animals with similar features

stubby—thick and short in length

READ MORE

Clay, Kathryn. *Triceratops and Other Horned Dinosaurs.* Dinosaur Fact Dig. North Mankato, Minn.: Capstone Press, 2016.

Johnson, Jinny. *Armored Dinosaurs.* Discovering Dinosaurs. Mankato, Minn.: Smart Apple Media, 2014.

Silverman, Buffy. *Can You Tell a Triceratops from a Protoceratops?* Dinosaur Look-Alikes. Minneapolis: Lerner Publications Company, 2014.

INTERNET SITES

FactHound offers a safe, fun way to find internet sites related to this book. All of the sites on FactHound have been researched by our staff.

Here's all you do:
Visit www.facthound.com
Type in this code: 9781479587681

Super-cool stuff!

Check out projects, games and lots more at
www.capstonekids.com

INDEX

BOOKS IN THE SERIES

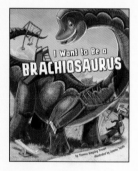
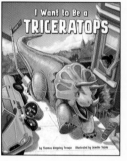
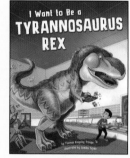
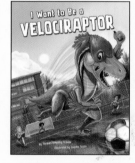

Dedication

To Travis, who can be as hard-headed as a triceratops!

Thanks to our adviser for his expertise, research, and advice:
Mathew J. Wedel, PhD
Associate Professor
Western University of Health Services

Editors: Christopher Harbo and Anna Butzer
Designer: Sarah Bennett
Art Director: Ashlee Suker
Production Specialist: Kathy McColley

The illustrations in this book were planned with pencil on paper and finished with digital paints.

Picture Window Books are published by Capstone,
1710 Roe Crest Drive, North Mankato, Minnesota 56003
www.capstonepub.com

Library of Congress Cataloging-in-Publication Data
Catalogue-in-publication information is on file with the Library of Congress.

ISBN 978-1-4795-8768-1 (library binding)
ISBN 978-1-4795-8772-8 (eBook PDF)

Summary: Follows two young girls as they transform into Triceratops and experience life from a dinosaur's perspective.

Printed and bound in the USA.
009685F16